I0186224

The Old-Time Radio Trivia Book V

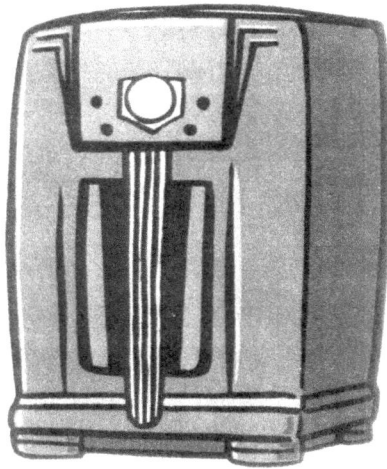

ALSO BY MEL SIMONS:

The Old-Time Radio Trivia Book

The Old-Time Television Trivia Book

Old-Time Radio Memories

The Show-Biz Trivia Book

Old-Time Television Memories

The Movie Trivia Book

Voices From the Philco

The Good Music Trivia Book

The Mel Simons Joke Book

The Old-Time Radio Trivia Book II

The Comedians Trivia Book

The Old-Time Radio Trivia Book III

Take These Jokes Please

The Old-Time Radio Trivia Book IV

The Old-Time Television Trivia Book II

The Old-Time Radio Trivia Book V

by Mel Simons

BearManor Media
2017

The Old-Time Radio Trivia Book V

© 2017 Mel Simons

All rights reserved.

For information, address:

BearManor Media
P. O. Box 71426
Albany, GA 31708

bearmanormedia.com

Typesetting and layout by John Teehan

Published in the USA by BearManor Media

ISBN — 978-1-62933-154-6

Dedication

This book is dedicated to my pal, Garo Hagopian.
Garo produced many of my radio shows on WBZ.
He is now a top newscaster on the station.
We both share the love of old-time radio.

Mel Simons
www.melsimons.net

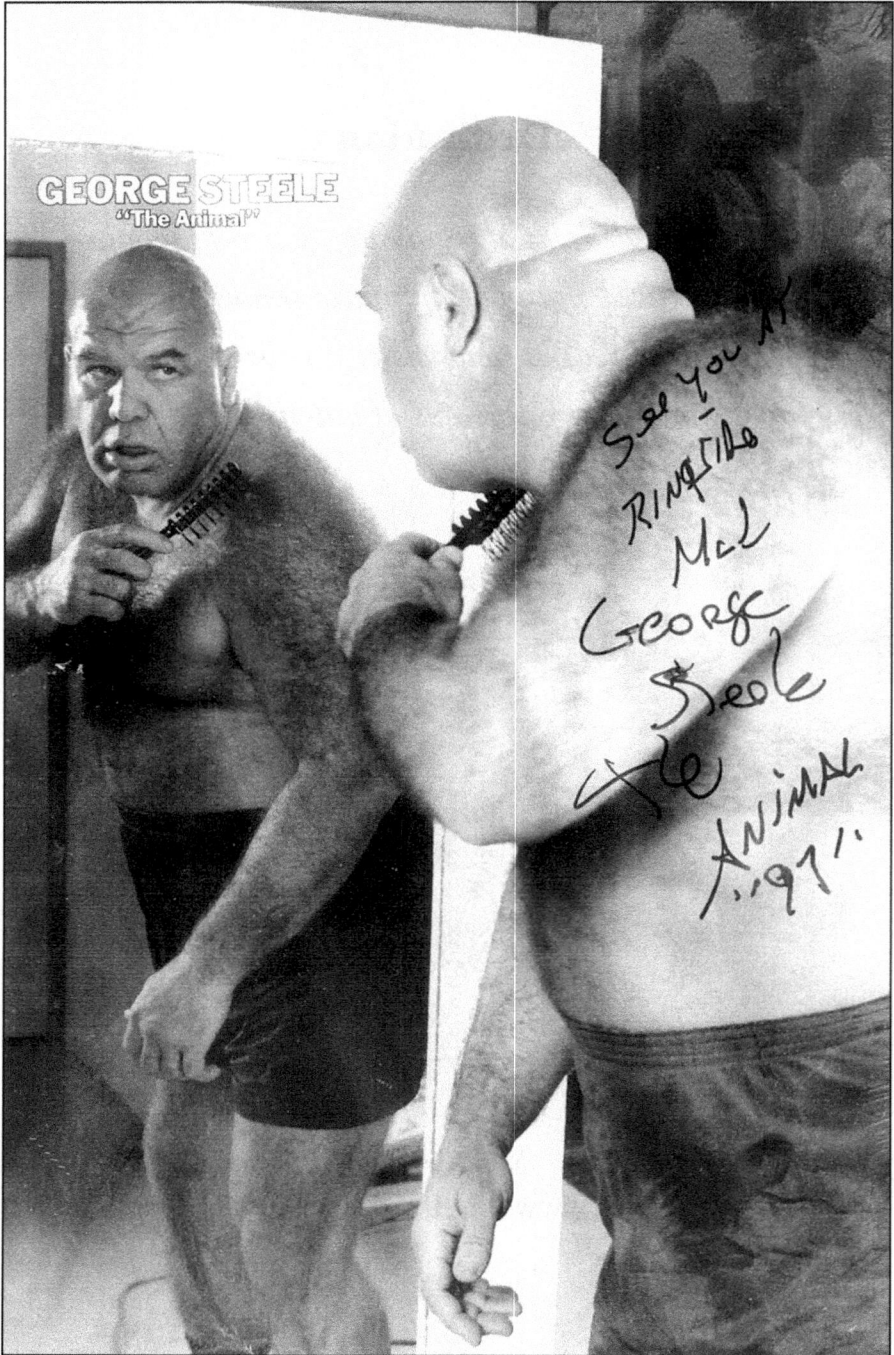

George 'The Animal' Steele

Foreword

MEL SIMONS AND I come from two different worlds but we have been friends for many years. I had a great career as a heavyweight wrestler and was known as George "The Animal" Steele. Mel is an entertainer, radio personality, MC and devotee of Old-Time Radio and Television and is known as "The King of Nostalgia." We crossed paths when Mel announced wrestling matches. When Mel started writing Radio and TV nostalgia books, my wife and I would love leafing through them to relive the amazing "good old days of radio." He enriched our knowledge and brought back wonderful memories of our early years.

Mel gives us a blast from the past once again with *The Old-Time Radio Trivia Book V*. Be sure to read all of his books and share them with your friends and family. They include great facts, figures and autographs that make for great reads and they offer fun for everyone.

– George "The Animal" Steele

George 'The Animal' Steel and Mel Simons

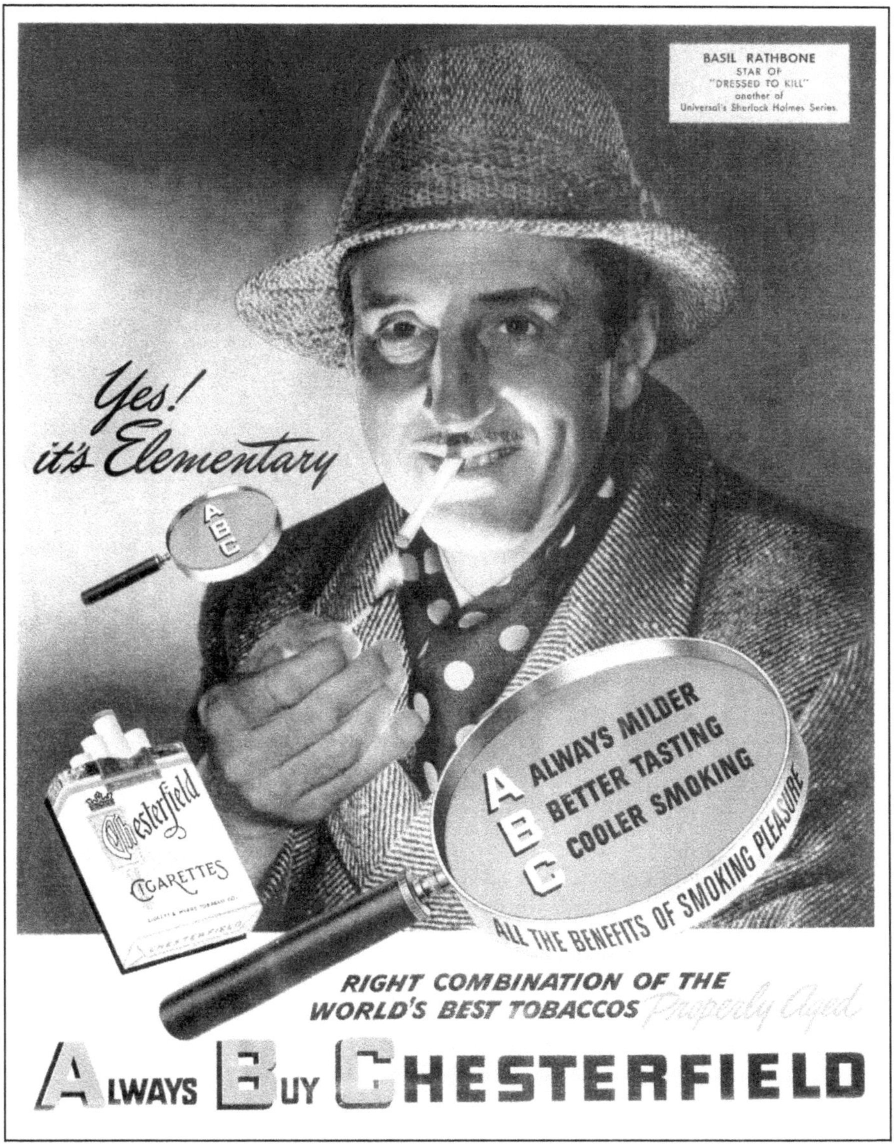

Basil Rathbone

(L to R) George Jessel – Eddie Cantor – George Burns – Jack Benny

GEORGE JESSEL

George was the first comedian in vaudeville to use a telephone as a prop. He starred on Broadway in a dramatic production of The Jazz Singer. President Harry Truman named George "The Toastmaster General of the United States."

EDDIE CANTOR

Eddie became a major star in "The Ziegfeld Follies." He then turned to radio, where he was popular for twenty-six years. Eddie appeared once a month of TV's Colgate Comedy Hour. He often joked about his wife Ida and their five daughters.

GEORGE BURNS

One of the most popular comedians in vaudeville, radio and television, he always played straight man to his wife Gracie. He always held a cigar in his hand. George won the Academy Award for Best Supporting Actor in the movie The Sunshine Boys.

JACK BENNY

He was the greatest comedian during The Golden Days of Radio. He owned Sunday nights. Jack was known for having the best timing in the business. His great love was playing the violin. Jack was married to Mary Livingstone for many years.

George Burns and Gracie Allen

Quiz #1

GENERAL QUESTIONS
(Answers on page 117)

1. Name the Great Gildersleeve's niece.

2. Ted Collins was the host of which radio show?

3. Jerry Colonna was a second banana to what comedian?

4. Name the operator on *Fibber McGee & Molly*.

5. Where did Our Gal Sunday live?

6. What was the name of Jack Benny's parrot?

7. Who was known as the Toastmaster General of the United States?

8. Name the long-time sponsor of *The Lone Ranger*.

9. The Man in Black hosted which radio show?

10. On *The Fred Allen Show*, who played Mr. Moody?

Bill Cullen

Quiz #2

WOMEN OF LAUGHTER
Match the comedienne with the show
(Answers on page 117)

1. Marie Wilson
2. Gale Storm
3. Eve Arden
4. Minnie Pearl
5. Audrey Totter
6. Ann Sothern
7. Mary Livingstone
8. Lulu McConnell
9. Janet Waldo
10. Gertrude Berg

a. *Meet Millie*
b. *Grand Old Opry*
c. *The Goldbergs*
d. *Maisie*
e. *The Jack Benny Show*
f. *My Little Margie*
g. *Meet Corliss Archer*
h. *Our Miss Brooks*
i. *It Pays To Be Ignorant*
j. *My Friend Irma*

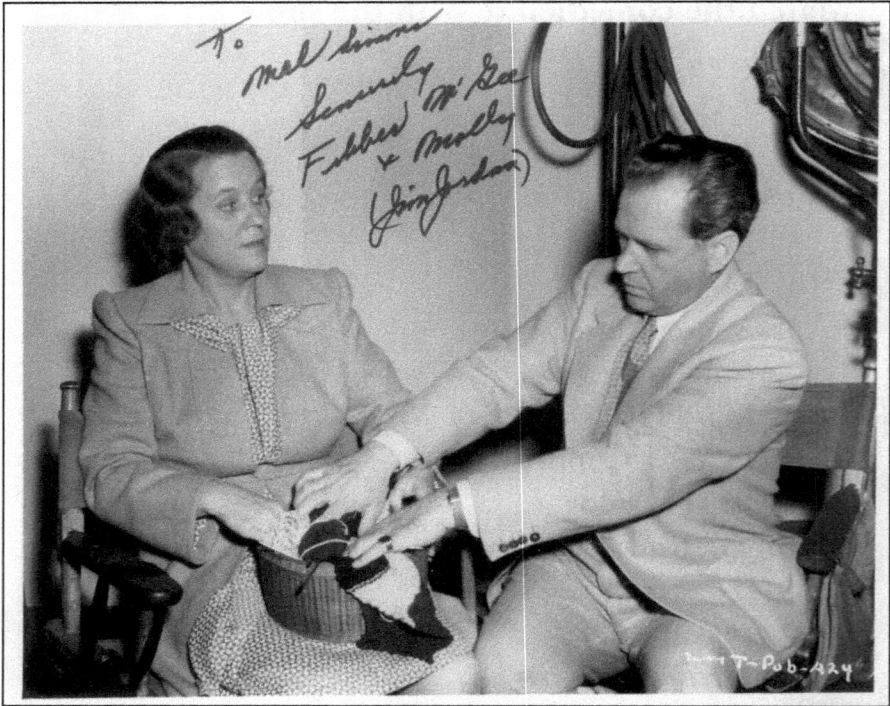

Fibber McGee and Molly

(L to R) Fred Foy – Mel Simons – Raymond Edward Johnson

Quiz #3

FILL IN THE RADIO SHOW
(Answers on Page 118)

1. Look, up in the sky! It's a bird! It's a plane! It's
_____.

2. A tale well calculated to keep you in _____.

3. There he goes, into that drug store. _____
_____.

4. Oh, Pancho _____ _____ _____.

5. The kindly old investigator _____ _____,
_____ _____ _____.

6. It is later than you think _____ _____.

7. _____ _____ Brought to you every day by
the makers of Ovaltine.

8. Time now for _____ _____ _____
_____ _____.

9. Good evening friends of the _____ _____.

10. This is _____ _____ _____, inviting
you to join me on another journey into the strange
and terrifying.

Benny Goodman

Marie Wilson – Cy Howard – John Brown. My Friend Irma

Sheldon Leonard

Quiz #4

SOAP OPERA THEME SONGS
Match the soap with its theme.
(Answers on Page 118)

1. *Our Gal Sunday*
2. *Pepper Young's Family*
3. *The Goldbergs*
4. *Aunt Jenny's True Life Stories*
5. *Myrt and Marge*
6. *Against the Storm*
7. *Mary Marlin*
8. *Joyce Jordan, Girl Intern*
9. *Stella Dallas*
10. *Backstage Wife*

a. "Poor Butterfly"
b. "Red River Valley"
c. "Poeme"
d. "Rose of Tralee"
e. "Au Matin"
f. "Clair de lune"
g. "Toselli's Serenade"
h. "Believe Me If All Those Endearing Young Charms"
i. "Ich liebe"
j. "How Can I Leave Thee"

Chester Lauck and Norris Goff. Lum and Abner

Paul Whiteman

Quiz #5

MULTIPLE CHOICE
(Answers on Page 118)

1. The *Quiz Kids* radio show took place in what city?
   a) Chicago b) New York c) Los Angeles

2. Rod O'Connor was the announcer on whose show?
   a) Jack Carson b) Bob Hope c) Red Skelton

3. The Walking Man appeared on what show?
   a) *Suspense* b) *Truth or Consequences*
   c) *The Red Skelton Show*

4. Who was The Walking Man?
   a) Boris Karloff b) Jack Benny c) Peter Lorre

5. Parkyakarkus was played by whom?
   a) Bert Gordon b) Bill Dana c) Harry Einstein

6. Frances Langford and Don Ameche starred on which show?
   a) *The Bickersons* b) *All in the Family* c) *Betty Boop*

7. Ish Kabibble's real name was –
   a) Harry Babbitt b) Mervyn Bogue
   c) Mike Douglas

8. The host of *The Kraft Music Hall* was –
   a) Bing Crosby b) Eddie Cantor c) Al Jolson

9. Name the mayor who read the Sunday comic strips.
   a) Major Curley b) Mayor Beame
   c) Mayor LaGuardia

10. Who was known as "The King of Jazz"?
    a) Tommy Dorsey b) Paul Whiteman
    c) Jimmy Dorsey

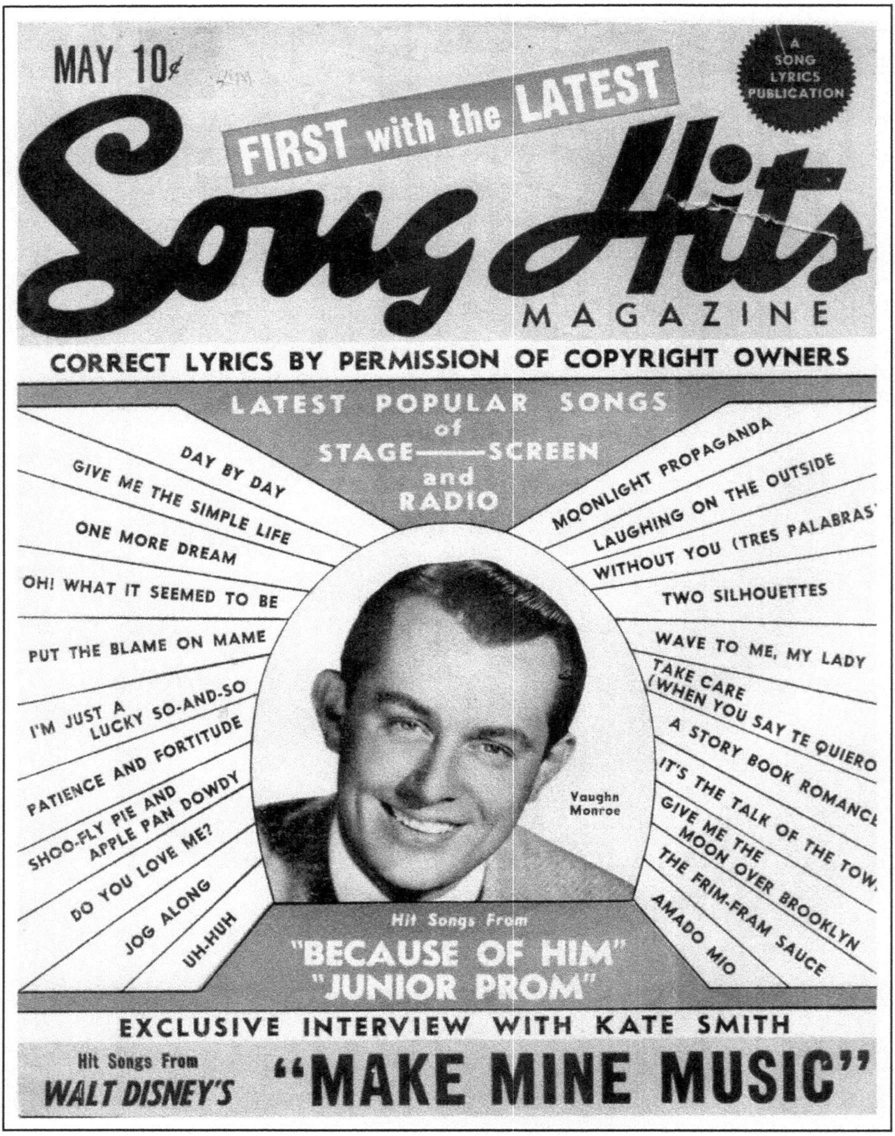

Vaughn Monroe

Quiz #6

TRUE OR FALSE
(Answers on Page 119)

1. *The Big Show* was hosted by Tallulah Bankhead.

2. Don Ameche and Jim Ameche were cousins.

3. Randy Stone was a reporter for *The Chicago Star*.

4. Nora Drake played the role of a doctor.

5. Louella Parsons and Hedda Hopper were rivals on radio and newspaper.

6. *The Shadow*'s longest-running sponsor was Ajax.

7. Sgt. Preston's first name was Bob.

8. *The Saint*'s real name was Simon Templar.

9. *Cavalcade of America* was sponsored by DuPont.

10. Herbert Marshall was the star of *A Man Called X.*

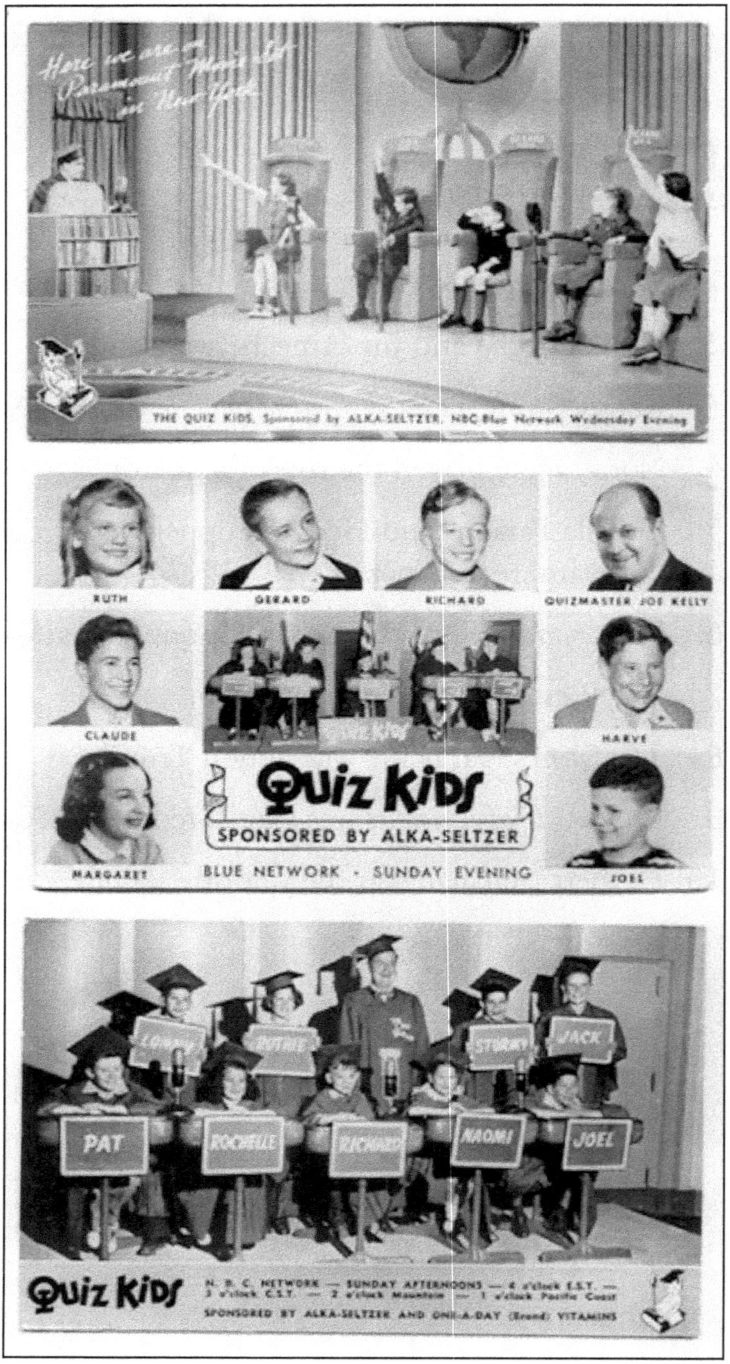

The Quiz Kids

Richard Kollmar – Boston Blackie

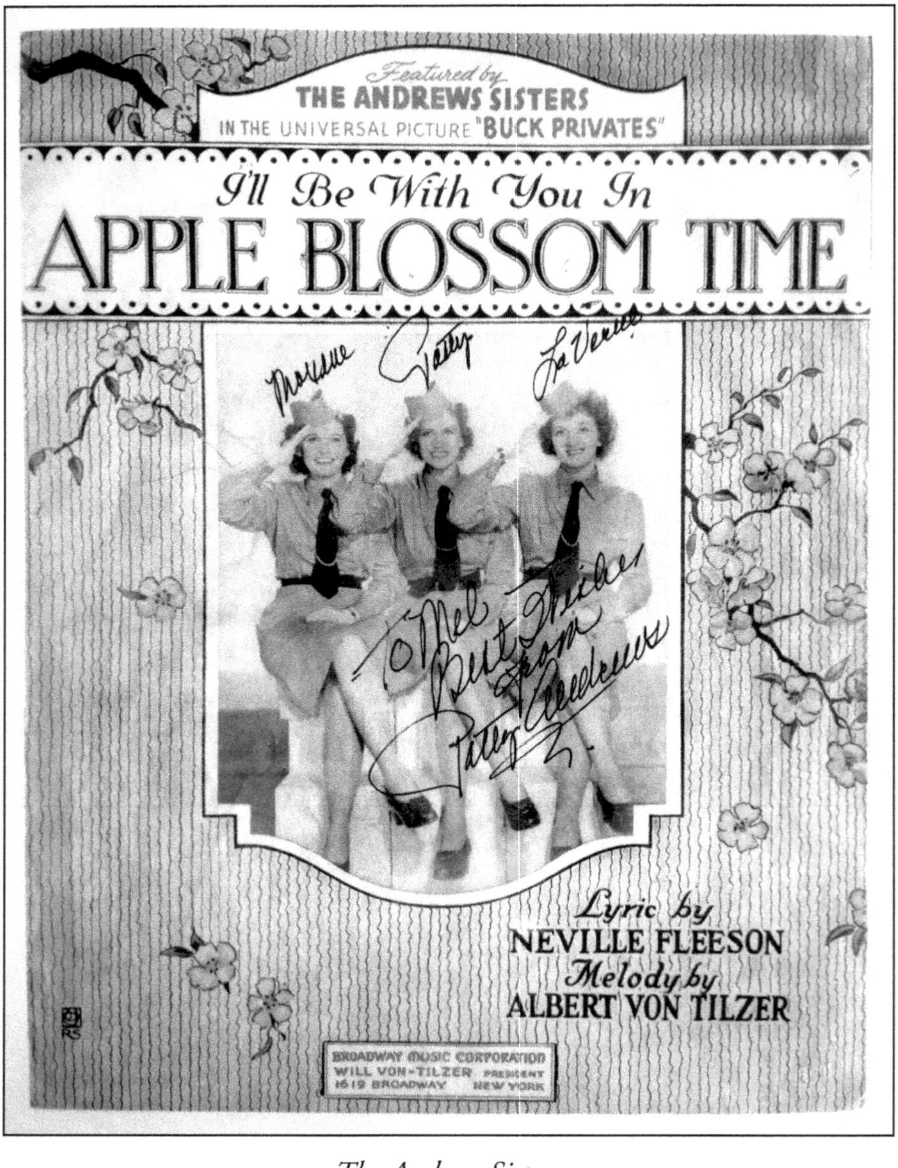

The Andrew Sisters

Lon Clark – Nick Carter and Bret Morrison – The Shadow

The cast of Gunsmoke *(left to right) Howard McNear - William Conrad - Georgia Ellis - Parley Baer*

Quiz #7

GUNSMOKE
(Answers on Page 119)

1. *Gunsmoke* was called what type of Western?

2. What was Matt Dillon's profession?

3. What was the name of his deputy?

4. Who played the deputy?

5. Georgia Ellis played what character?

6. What did she do for a living?

7. Howard McNear played what character?

8. Where did the show take place?

9. Who played the music?

10. Name the producer-director of the show.

The first Great Gildersleeve, Hal Peary

The second Great Gildersleeve, Willard Waterman

Quiz #8

MATCH THE RADIO STAR WITH THE MOVIE

(Answers on Page 119)

1. Orson Welles
2. Red Skelton
3. Ronald Coleman
4. Walter Winchell
5. Jackie Gleason
6. Ed Wynn
7. The Andrews Sisters
8. Frank Sinatra
9. Alice Faye
10. Steve Allen

a. *The Hustler*
b. *A Double Life*
c. *The Benny Goodman Story*
d. *High Society*
e. *Citizen Kane*
f. *Rose of Washington Square*
g. *The Diary of Anne Frank*
h. *In the Navy*
i. *The Fuller Brush Man*
j. *Wake Up and Live*

Bob Crosby

George Fenneman

Patti Page

Quiz #9

MATCH THE DETECTIVE SHOW WITH THE ACTOR

(Answers on Page 120)

1. *Dragnet*
2. *Mr. District Attorney*
3. *Charlie Chan*
4. *The Saint*
5. *A Man Called X*
6. *Nero Wolfe*
7. *David Harding, Counterspy*
8. *Johnny Dollar*
9. *Man Against Crime*
10. *Dangerous Assignment*

a. Sydney Greenstreet
b. Vincent Price
c. Ralph Bellamy
d. Brian Donlevy
e. Jack Webb
f. Herbert Marshall
g. Jay Jostyn
h. Ed Begley
i. Bob Bailey
j. Don MacLaughlin

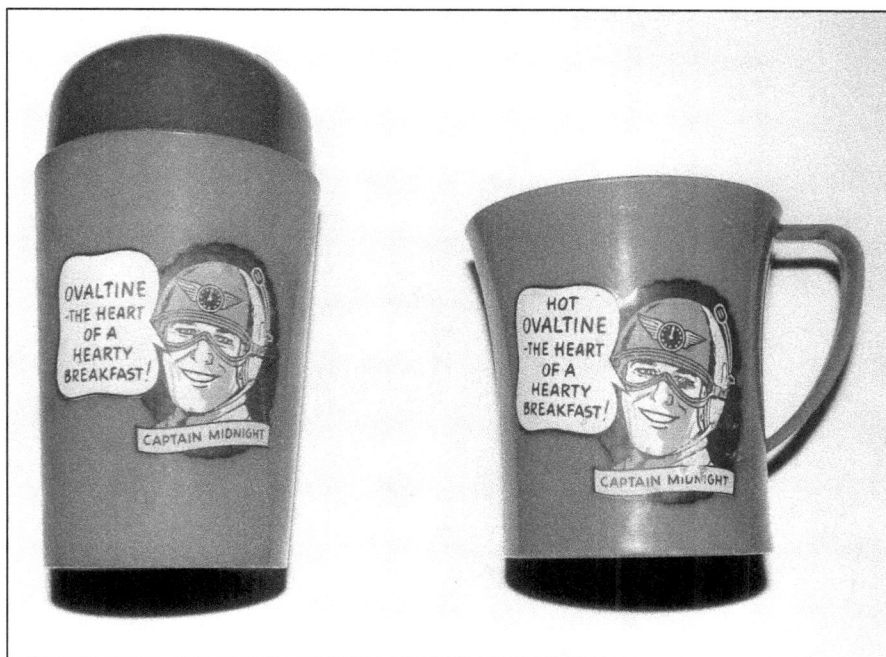

Captain Midnight Shake-Up Mug and Cup

Jack Benny and Bob Hope

(L to R) Oscar Levant – Ken Carpenter – Al Jolson, Kraft Music Hall

Bob Elliott and Mel Simons

Quiz #10

BOB AND RAY
(Answers on Page 120)

1. What are Bob's and Ray's last names?

2. They began their careers on what Boston radio station?

3. Name the New York radio station that they were on.

4. They did a famous commercial for what beer?

5. What was the parody they did for *One Man's Family*?

6. Who was their news reporter?

7. Name their Broadway show.

8. Who was the lady they often featured?

9. What was the parody they did for Mary Noble, Backstage Wife?

10. They always ended their show saying what?

Don Dunphy

Jay Jostyn – Mr. District Attorney

Quiz #11

SONGS PLAYED ON THE RADIO
Fill in the color
(Answers on Page 120)

1. "_____ Roses For a _____ Lady"

2. "When Your Hair Has Turned to _____"

3. "Out of an _____ Colored Sky"

4. "_____ Tree, Very Pretty"

5. "Beautiful, Beautiful _____ Eyes, I'll Never Love _____ Eyes Again"

6. "Sweet _____, Sweeter Than the Roses"

7. "_____ Tambourine"

8. "_____ Shoelaces"

9. "We All Live in a _____ Submarine"

10. "Deep _____"

Ed Wynn

Quiz #12

MULTIPLE CHOICE
(Answers on Page 121)

1. Who was the host of *The Mysterious Traveler?*
   a) Maurice Tarplin b) The Man in Black
   c) Raymond

2. What was Young Widder Brown's first name?
   a) Joan b) Ellen c) Marcia

3. What instrument did Jacques Bernard play?
   a) Violin b) piano c) trombone

4. Who played Tom Mix on radio?
   a) Tom Mix b) Fred Foy c) Curley Bradley

5. Name the high school that Jack Armstrong attended.
   a) Middlesex High b) Riverdale High
   c) Hudson High

6. Name the character that John Dehner played on
   Have Gun, Will Travel.
   a) Smokey b) Paladin c) Tex

7. Who was the dean on *The Kollege of Musical Knowledge?*
   a) Paul Whiteman b) Kay Kyser
   c) Tommy Dorsey

8. Name the long-time sponsor of *Richard Diamond.*
   a) Rexall b) Mott's Apple Juice c) Ipana

9. Frances Octavia Smith is the real name of who?
   a) Gracie Allen b) Marie Wilson c) Dale Evans

10. Who was the magic detective?
    a) Blackstone b) Houdini c) Dunninger

TONIGHT!
PEPSODENT'S
HERBERT MARSHALL
in
THE MAN CALLED "X"
Tune In Every Tuesday
8 P. M.—WTMJ
Tonight
America's greatest hit-maker sings your hit songs!
"KATE SMITH SINGS"
Produced & Directed by TED COLLINS
7:30 · WISN
JEAN HERSHOLT
IN
"DR. CHRISTIAN"
Presented by the makers of
VASELINE
PREPARATIONS
7:00 P.M. ★ KIRO
SPARKLING NEW SUMMER SHOW!
HARRY JAMES
AND HIS MUSIC MAKERS
EVERY FRIDAY!
9:30 P. M. WISN
PRESENTED BY
Pabst Blue Ribbon Beer

Radio ads

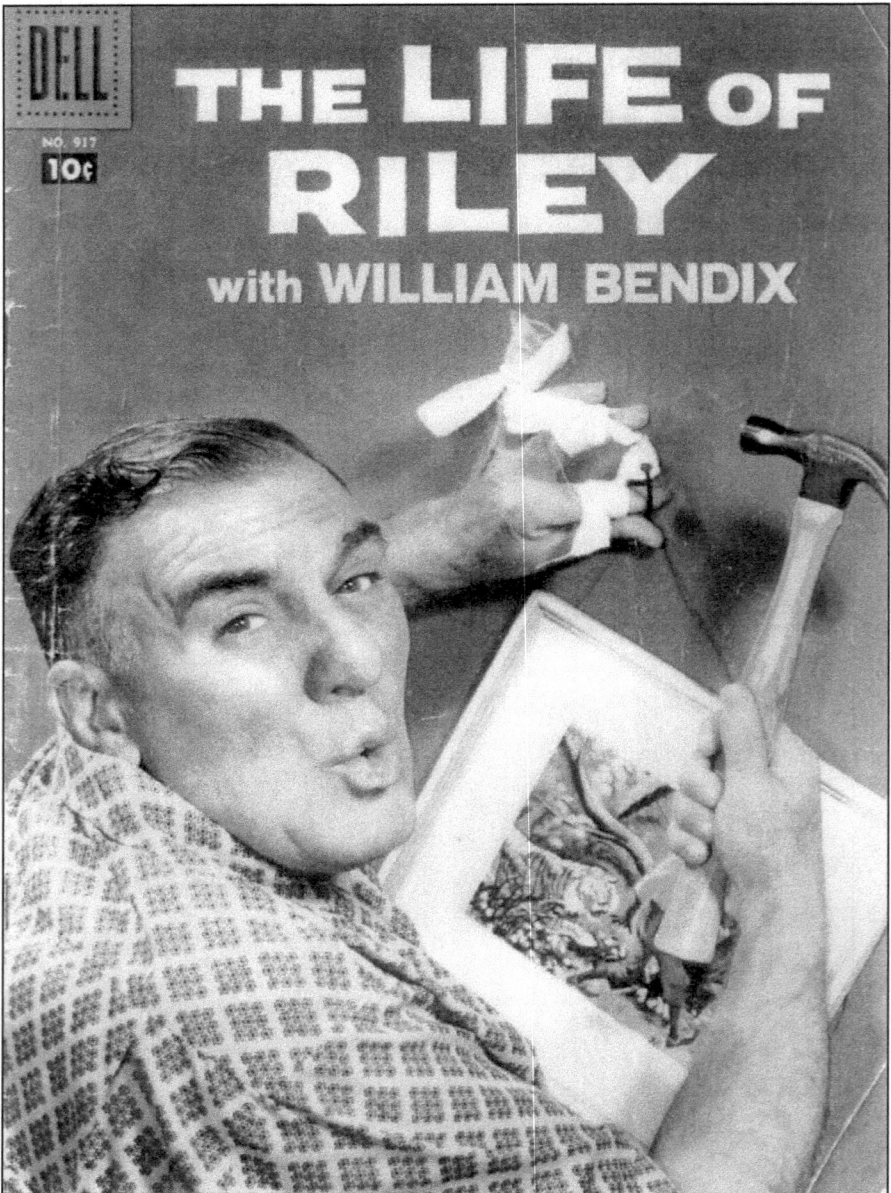

William Bendix

Top: *Eve Arden – Our Miss Brooks,*
Bottom: *Guy Madison and Andy Devine – Wild Bill Hickok*

Lanny Ross

Quiz #13

MATCH THE NAMES WITH THEIR RELATIONSHIP

(Answers on Page 121)

1. Ozzie to Ricky
2. Molly to Rosalie
3. Amos to Andy
4. Eddie to Ida
5. Pasquale to Luigi
6. Bud to Lou
7. Gracie to George
8. Babs to Chester
9. Dennis to Jack
10. Gildy to Marjorie

a. Husband
b. Daughter
c. Singer
d. Landlord
e. Father
f. Uncle
g. Mother
h. Friend
i. Wife
j. Partner

Captain Midnight Decoders

Little Orphan Annie Decoders

Quiz #14

GENERAL QUESTIONS
(Answers on Page 121)

1. Where did the Fat Man always weigh himself?

2. Bill Kenny was the lead singer for what vocal group?

3. Arch Obler created what show?

4. Who was My Friend Irma's landlady?

5. Name the cereal that was shot from guns.

6. On the show *Truth or Consequences*, who was The Walking Man?

7. Who played Tom Mix on radio?

8. Name Groucho's long-time announcer.

9. George Burns won the Academy Award for what movie?

10. Name two shows that Phil Harris appeared on.

Quiz #15

CAPTAIN MIDNIGHT
(Answers on Page 122)

1. Who sponsored the show?
2. What did Captain Midnight do for a living?
3. When and what time was the show on?
4. Name his two most famous premiums.
5. What was the captain's last name?
6. Captain Midnight was the leader of what group?
7. Who was the Captain's #1 enemy?
8. Name this enemy's daughter.
9. Who were his junior assistants?
10. What was Ichabod Mudd's nickname?

Quiz #16

DETECTIVE SHOWS

From the following list of detective shows:
5 appeared on radio
5 appeared on television
5 appeared on both
Who appeared on what?

(Answers on Page 122)

1. *Dragnet*
2. *Law and Order*
3. *The Mentalist*
4. *The Fat Man*
5. *Boston Blackie*
6. *Sam Spade*
7. *Kojak*
8. *Richard Diamond*
9. *Man Against Crime*
10. *Mr. Keen*
11. *Mr. Chamelion*
12. *Mr. District Attorney*
13. *Nick Carter*
14. *NYPD Blue*
15. *Streets of San Francisco*

Ed Gardner (Duffy's Tavern) and The Lone Ranger

The Mills Brothers

Quiz #17

OCCUPATIONS
Match the character with his or her occupation
(Answers on Page 123)

1. Matt Dillon
2. Sky King
3. Connie Brooks
4. Sam Spade
5. Britt Reid
6. Ozzie Nelson
7. Helen Trent
8. J. C. Dithers
9. Sgt. Preston
10. Larry Noble

a. School teacher
b. Actor
c. Newspaper publisher
d. U. S. Marshall
e. Canadian Mountie
f. Pilot
g. Nothing
h. Owner of a construction company
i. Private investigator
j. Wardrobe worker

Roy Rogers

Quiz #18

ROY ROGERS
(Answers on Page 123)

1. Who was Roy married to?

2. What was the name of Pat Brady's Jeep?

3. Name Roy's first vocal group.

4. What was their biggest hit record?

5. Name Roy's second vocal group.

6. What was Roy's theme song?

7. Who wrote the song?

8. Who was Buttermilk?

9. Roy made movies for what movie company?

10. What did Roy always say at the end of the show?

Radio ads

Sandra Gould – Duffy's Tavern – *A Date With Judy*

Penny Arcade cards

Quiz #19

GENERAL QUESTIONS
(Answers on Page 123)

1. Who was the master detective?

2. Jack Webb starred in what show before he did *Dragnet*?

3. Who created Perry Mason?

4. What branch of the service was Popeye in?

5. Name the show that began with a gong?

6. Who wrote "The Easy Aces"?

7. Jack Benny's professional radio debut was on what show?

8. Who said, "Up, up and away?"

9. What soft drink hits the spot?

10. Who replaced Howard Duff on Sam Spade?

Big Little Books

Bert Gordon (The Mad Russian) and Eddie Cantor

Quiz #20

MULTIPLE CHOICE
(Answers on Page 124)

1. *Quick As a Flash* was on what night of the week?
   a) Friday b) Saturday c) Sunday

2. Portland Hoffs was born in what city?
   a) Portland, Oregon b) Portland, Maine
   c) Portland, Ohio

3. Who was the Arkansas Traveler?
   a) Bob Burns b) Herb Shriner c) Will Rogers

4. Name the dog that did not star in a radio show.
   a) Lassie b) Rin Tin Tin c) Asta

5. Allan Jones' theme song was what?
   a) "Always" b) "The Donkey Serenade"
   c) "The Jones Boy"

6. Wendy Warren was played by whom?
   a) Cathy Lewis b) Florence Freeman
   c) Anne Seymour

7. Who was Singing Sam?
   a) Sam Jones b) Jay Hickerson c) Harry Frankel

8. Norman Brokenshire was best known as what?
   a) Announcer b) trumpet player c) singer

9. Santos Ortega played what detective?
   a) Nero Wolfe b) Charlie Chan
   c) Bulldog Drummond

10. Alan Reed's real name was what?
    a) Teddy Bergman b) Britt Reed c) Bob Forrest

Alan Young

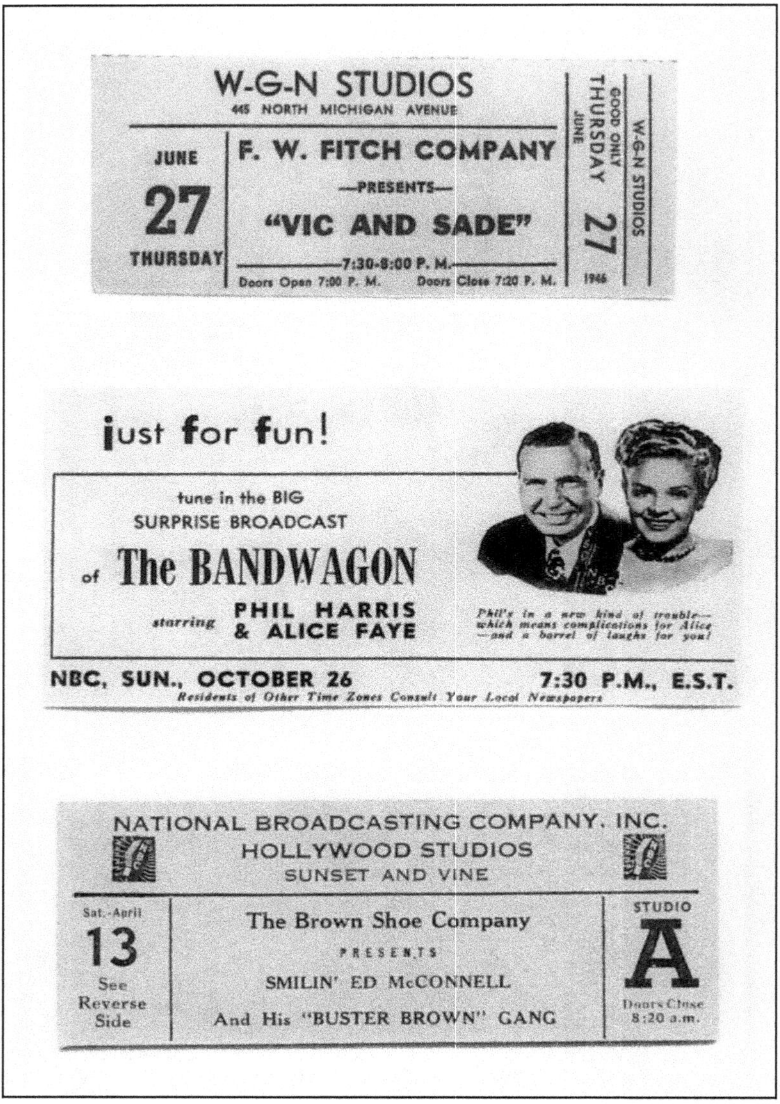

Tickets to radio shows

J. Scott Smart – The Fat Man

Quiz #21

MATCH THE SAYING WITH THE RADIO PERSONALITY

(Answers on Page 124)

1. "Mr. Allen, Mr. Allen"
2. "Thank you, music lovers"
3. "Howdeeee"
4. "Say the secret word . . ."
5. "I'm a bad boy."
6. "Gee whiz, Henry, gee whiz"
7. "Lotions of Love"
8. "Good evening from Hollywood"
9. "Vas you dere, Sharlie?"
10. "Duffy ain't here."

a. Groucho Marx
b. Walter Winchell
c. Portland Hoffa
d. Archie, the manager
e. Louella Parsons
f. Lou Costello
g. Minnie Pearl
h. Homer Brown
i. Spike Jones
j. Jack Pearl

The Green Hornet

BING CROSBY
on
PHILCO RADIO TIME
tonight
8.30 - 9.00
CKRM, 980
Every Thursday
BOWMAN BROTHERS LIMITED
Provincial Distributors
Regina and Saskatoon
LISTEN and LAUGH
WITH
Rexall DRUGS
Jimmy Durante
AND
Garry Moore
ON WISN
TONIGHT AT 9
New Laugh Time!
Ozzie & Harriet
TONIGHT
7:30 to 8:00 p.m.
CKRM
and every
Friday Night
Presented by
The International Silver Co.
of Canada, Limited
TONIGHT! TONIGHT!
JACK BENNY TIME!
WITH MARY LIVINGSTON
PHIL HARRIS • ROCHESTER
LARRY STEVENS • DON WILSON
PRESENTED BY
LUCKY STRIKE
L.S./M.F.T.
EVERY SUNDAY
WTMJ
6 P.M.

Radio ads

(L to R) Dennis Day – Mel Simons – Don Wilson

The cast of Pepper Young's family sitting down to breakfast (left to right) Hattie (serving), mother Mary Young, Peggy, Carter Trent, Sam Young and Pepper himself

Ezra Stone – The Aldrich Family

Jackie Kelk – Superman *and* The Aldrich Family

Lucille Ball – My Favorite Husband

Quiz #22

SONGS PLAYED ON RADIO'S *YOUR HIT PARADE*
Match the song with who had the hit record
(Answers on Page 124)

1. "All or Nothing At All"
2. "The Anniversary Song"
3. "Paper Doll"
4. "To Each His Own"
5. "The Gypsy"
6. "Darling, Jo Vous Aime Beaucoup"
7. "My Foolish Heart"
8. "A Tree in the Meadow"
9. "Careless Hands"
10. "Some Enchanted Evening"

a. Ezio Pinza
b. Mel Torme
c. The Ink Spots
d. Frank Sinatra
e. Billy Eckstine
f. Hildegarde
g. The Mills Brothers
h. Margaret Whiting
i. Al Jolson
j. Tony Martin

Quiz #23

MATCH THE SAYING WITH THE RADIO PERSONALITY

(Answers on Page 125)

1. "Mortimer, how can you be so stupid?"
2. "That's a joke, son."
3. "Good evening, opera lovers from coast to coast"
4. "This way, Pancho, vamonos"
5. "Who's on first, what's on second, I don't know's on third."
6. "Just the facts, ma'am."
7. "I'm feeling mighty low."
8. "Kids say the darnedest things."
9. "I know many strange tales hidden in the hearts of men and women."
10. "Monkeys is the qwaziest people."

a. The Cisco Kid
b. Sgt. Joe Friday
c. Art Linkletter
d. The Whistler
e. Senator Claghorn
f. Edgar Bergen
g. Lou Lehr
h. Milton Cross
i. Bud Abbott
j. Candy Dandido

Quiz #24

RELATIONSHIPS
Match the relationship
(Answers on Page 125)

1. Roy and Dale
2. Osgood and Connie
3. Birdie and Throckmorton
4. Oscar and Al
5. Ethelbert and Casey
6. Cookie and Dagwood
7. Champion and Gene
8. Jane and Goodman
9. Myrt and Fibber
10. Ted and Kate

a. Maid
b. Horse
c. Daughter
d. Principal
e. Operator
f. Wife
g. Pianist
h. Bartender
i. Announcer
j. Husband

Quiz #25

MATCH THE RADIO STAR WITH THE MOVIE
(Answers on Page 125)

1. Bing Crosby
2. Martin and Lewis
3. Lucille Ball
4. Kay Kyser
5. Jean Hersholt
6. William Bendix
7. Rudy Vallee
8. Amos 'n' Andy
9. Louella Parsons
10. Groucho Marx

a. *The Vagabond Lover*
b. *My Favorite Spy*
c. *Going My Way*
d. *Check and Double Check*
e. *Mame*
f. *A Day at the Races*
g. *Hollywood Hotel*
h. *The Babe Ruth Story*
i. *Meet Dr. Christian*
j. *At War With the Army*

SUPERMAN
IS ON
THE RADIO!
SPONSORED BY THE MAKERS OF FORCE OVER THE FOLLOWING STATIONS

The SHADOW KNOWS
JOHN MANN & SONS
323 Colborne St. Brantford
Phone 90
'blue coal'
THE WORLD'S FINEST ANTHRACITE

Radio ads

Janet Waldo – Meet Corliss Archer

The cast of The Jack Benny Show

Quiz #26

TRUE OR FALSE
(Answers on Page 126)

1. Signal Oil sponsored *The Whistler.*

2. Chester Riley's wife was named Peg.

3. Inspector Faraday appeared on *The Fat Man.*

4. The star of *Masie* was Gale Storm.

5. Arch Obler was the host of *Inner Sanctum.*

6. Marion Seldes often appeared on *The CBS Mystery Theater.*

7. The song "Manhattan Serenade" was the theme song of Easy Aces.

8. Thorny was the next-door neighbor of Ozzie and Harriet.

9. *Suspense* was on radio for fifteen years.

10. Jack Benny once hosted the Academy Awards.

George Burns and Gracie Allen

Lon Clark and Charlotte Manson. Nick Carter, Master Detective

Quiz #27

SOAP OPERA THEME SONGS
Match the soap with its theme
(Answers on Page 126)

1. *One Man's Family*
2. *The Romance of Helen Trent*
3. *Big Sister*
4. *Hilltop House*
5. *Valiant Lady*
6. *The Road of Life*
7. *Lorenzo Jones*
8. *David Harum*
9. *Just Plain Bill*
10. *When a Girl Marries*

a. "Funiculi Funicula"
b. "Juanita"
c. "Journey Into Melody"
d. "Drigo's Serenade"
e. "Sunbonnet Sue"
f. "Valse Bluette"
g. "Brahm's Lullaby"
h. "Polly Wolly Doodle"
i. "Estrellita"
j. "Andante Cantabile"

Penny arcade cards

Quiz #28

CIGARETTE COMMERCIALS
Fill in the cigarette
(Answers on Page 126)

1. "_____ tastes good like a cigarette should."

2. "I'd walk a mile for a _____."

3. "Call for _____ _____."

4. "The taste of _____."

5. "You get a lot to like with a _____."

6. "Willie, the Penguin says, "Smoke _____."

7. "You can take _____ out of the country, but you can't take the country out of _____."

8. "_____ taste better, cleaner, fresher, smoother."

9. "_____ cigarettes, the pack with the coupon on the back."

10. "Smoke dreams, from smoke rings, while a _____ burns."

Jimmy Stewart – The Six Shooter

Quiz #29

RELATIONSHIPS
Match the relationship
(Answers on Page 127)

1. Eddie and Archie
2. Gil and Helen
3. Molly and Rosalie
4. Nick and Nora
5. Pancho and Cisco
6. Olive and Popeye
7. Edgar and Mortimer
8. Patsy and Nick
9. Dennis and Jack
10. Pasquale and Luigi

a. Landlord
b. Assistant
c. Girlfriend
d. Waiter
e. Mother
f. Singer
g. Ventriloquist
h. Sidekick
i. Husband
j. Boyfriend

Fred Foy

Bob Hastings (Archie Andrews) – Mel Simons –
Ivan Curry (Bobby Benson)

Penny arcade cards

Art Linkletter

(left to right) Bob Burns – Tommy Riggs – Charlie McCarthy –
Edgar Bergen – Rudy Vallee – Joe Penner

Quiz #30

MATCH THE ANNOUNCER WITH THE PROGRAM

(Answers on Page 127)

1. *The Green Hornet*
2. *The Whistler*
3. *Fred Allen*
4. *Dragnet*
5. *Metropolitan Opera*
6. *Suspense*
7. *Kraft Music Hall*
8. *Superman*
9. *Gunsmoke*
10. *Phil Harris – Alice Faye*

a. Kenny Delmar
b. The Man in Black
c. Fred Foy
d. George Fenneman
e. Jackson Beck
f. Milton Cross
g. Marvin Miller
h. Bill Forman
i. George Walsh
j. Ken Carpenter

Quiz #31

BIRTHPLACES
Match the radio star with his/her birthplace
(Answers on Page 127)

1. Jack Benny
2. Milton Berle
3. Kate Smith
4. Al Jolson
5. Fred Allen
6. Rudy Vallee
7. George Gershwin
8. Bert Parks
9. Joe Penner
10. Perry Como

a. St. Petersburg, Russia
b. Vermont
c. Chicago
d. New York, New York
e. Atlanta, Georgia
f. Canonsberg, Pennsylvania
g. Hungary
h. Cambridge, Massachusetts
i. Brooklyn, New York
j. Greenville, Virginia

Ed Gardner and Jimmy Durante

Red Skelton, Bob Hope, and Rudy Vallee

Quiz #32

ABBOTT AND COSTELLO
(Answers on Page 128)

1. What is Bud Abbott's real first name?

2. What is Lou Costello's real last name?

3. They were in what aspect of show business originally?

4. What's the best way to describe their comedy?

5. They got their start on whose radio show?

6. Who put them on that show?

7. What were Lou's opening words on their radio show?

8. Name their most famous comedy routine.

9. What was Lou's most famous line criticizing himself?

10. Name their first movie.

Jo Stafford

Quiz #33

TRUE OR FALSE
(Answers on Page 128)

1. Agnes Moorehead was known as "The First Lady of Suspense."

2. Oxydol sponsored *Ma Perkins*.

3. Carol Burnett once had her own radio show.

4. Richard Diamond, detective, always sang a song at the end of his show.

5. The long-time announcer for Bing Crosby was Harlow Wilcox.

6. Himan Brown created *The CBS Mystery Theater*.

7. Sgt. Preston's dog was named Bullet.

8. The Queen of the West was Dale Evans.

9. Portland Hoffa was named Portland because she was born in Portland, Oregon.

10. WXYZ was a radio station in Chicago.

Hopalong Cassidy

Quiz #34

BIRTHPLACES
Match the radio star with his/her birthplace
(Answers on Page 128)

1. Edgar Bergen
2. Bing Crosby
3. Alice Faye
4. Dean Martin
5. Ozzie Nelson
6. Gracie Allen
7. Guy Lombardo
8. Ed Wynn
9. Dick Powell
10. Nat "King" Cole

a. Steubenville, Ohio
b. Chicago, Illinois
c. Spokane, Washington
d. Jersey City, New Jersey
e. Philadelphia, Pennsylvania
f. San Francisco, California
g. London, Ontario, Canada
h. Mt. View, Arkansas
i. Montgomery, Alabama
j. New York, New York

Milton Berle and George Jessel

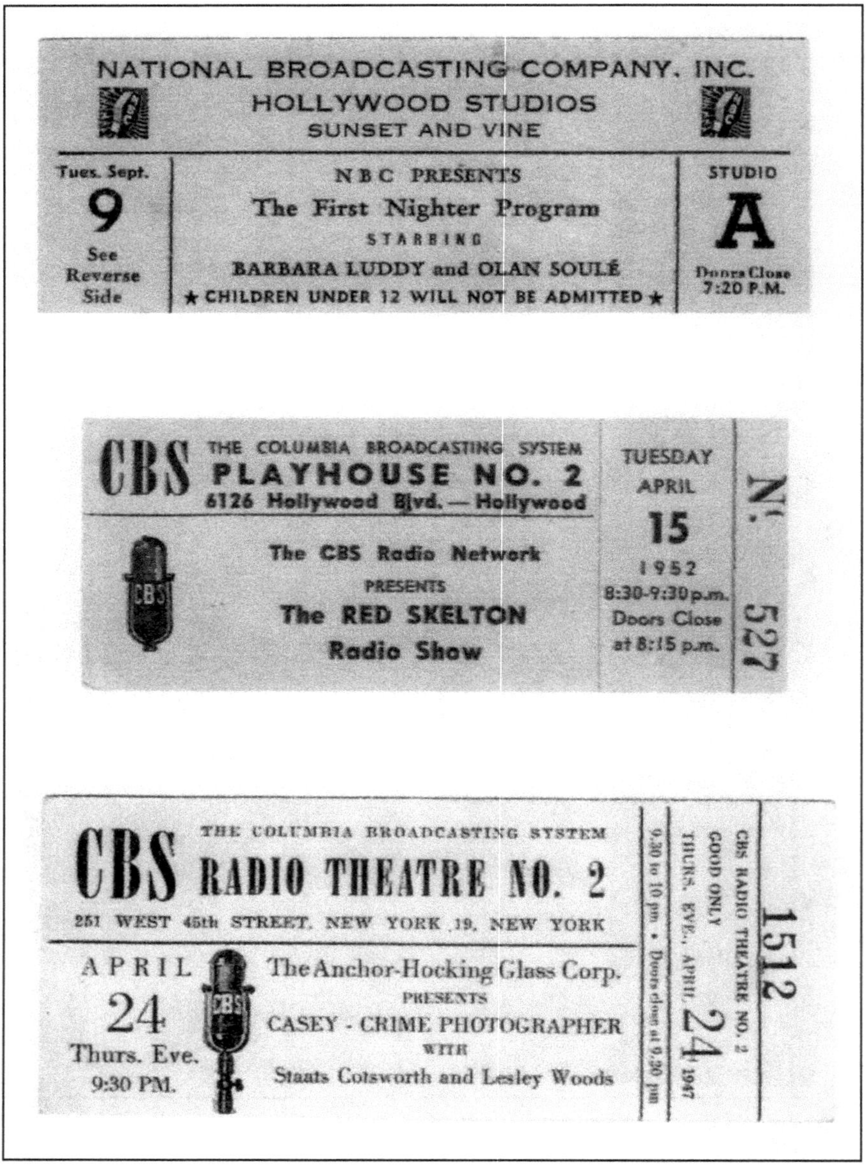

Tickets to radio shows

Quiz #35

MULTIPLE CHOICE
(Answers on Page 129)

1. Name the Shirley who starred in *Little Orphan Annie*.
   a) Shirley Bell b) Shirley Temple
   c) Shirley Mitchell

2. Who was known as "The Old Maestro"?
   a) Paul Whiteman b) Ben Bernie
   c) Lawrence Welk

3. What sport did Clem McCarthy not announce?
   a) horse racing b) boxing c) football

4. Don Ameche's brother was who?
   a) Charles b) Jim c) Barton

5. Dick Powell was once married to whom?
   a) June Allyson b) Ava Gardner c) Lauren Bacall

6. Who was Hopalong Cassidy's sidekick?
   a) Pat Brady b) Pat Buttram c) California Carlson

7. Who announced the Friday night fights?
   a) Bill Corum b) Howard Cosell c) Don Dunphy

8. How many children did Eddie Cantor have?
   a) four b) five c) six

9. Who said, "Call for Philip Morris"?
   a) Johnny b) Jimmy c) Philip

10. Who was the singing star of *The Railroad Hour*?
    a) Lanny Ross b) Gordon MacRae
    c) Nelson Eddy

Bing Crosby

Quiz #36

GENERAL QUESTIONS
(Answers on Page 129)

1. Who discovered Eddie Fisher?

2. Waterman's Pens and Sloan's Liniment sponsored what show?

3. Who played Rocky Fortune?

4. Name the long-time announcer on *Your Hit Parade*.

5. What was *Bob and Ray*'s closing line?

6. Who was known as the First Lady of Radio?

7. What brand of coffee sponsored George Burns and Gracie Allen?

8. Elliot Lewis was once married to what radio actress?

9. On the show *Let George Do It*, what was George's last name?

10. Who ended his show saying, "Good night to you, and I do mean you."

Arthur Godfrey

Quiz #37

DETECTIVE SHOWS
(Answers on Page 129)

1. Who created Sherlock Holmes?

2. Who was J. Scott Smart?

3. Mike Waring was known as whom?

4. What were the first names of Mr. and Mrs. North?

5. Name Nick Carter's adopted son.

6. Who was known as "The Man of Many Faces"?

7. William Gargan starred in which show?

8. Who was the kindly old investigator?

9. Who always said "Just the facts, Ma'am"?

10. Name the detective whose show opened with a fog horn and footsteps.

Big Little Books

Stan Freberg and Mel Simons

Quiz #38

MATCH THE SAYING WITH THE RADIO PERSONALITY

(Answers on Page 130)

1. "I take this same train every week."
2. "So you want to lead a band."
3. "Saints preserve us, Mr. Keen."
4. "Hiya kids, hiya, hiya."
5. "I have written a poem."
6. "Be good to yourself."
7. "You min it."
8. "Period, end of report."
9. "Cisco, the sheriff, he is getting closer."
10. "Evenin' folks, how y'all?"

a) Sam Spade
b) Mike Clancy
c) Don McNeil
d) The Mysterious Traveler
e) Pancho
f) Sammy Kaye
g) Kay Kyser
h) Froggy, the gremlin
i) The Mad Russian
j) Harry McNaughton

Freeman Gosden and Charles Correll – Amos 'n Andy

Quiz #39

TRUE OR FALSE
(Answers on Page 130)

1. Many of the early soap operas came from Chicago.

2. *Captain Kangaroo* was once on radio.

3. The first Mr. Hush was Jack Dempsey.

4. The featured singer on *The Railroad Hour* was Arthur Tracy.

5. Many of the big band remotes came from Frank Dailey's Meadowbrook.

6. Staats Cotsworth was the star of *Crime Club*.

7. Bob and Ray began their career on WHDH in Boston.

8. Brad Runyon was the Thin Man.

9. Henry Morgan was the son of Russ Morgan.

10. Dick Cavett began his career on radio.

Arthur Anderson – Let's Pretend

Quiz #40

MULTIPLE CHOICE
(Answers on Page 130)

1. Who played The Falcon?
a) Les Damon   b) Les Tremaine   c) Robert Dryden

2. Lorenzo Jones was married to whom?
a) Agnes   b) Barbara   c) Belle

3. Who was Al Goodman?
a) orchestra leader   b) comedian   c) emcee

4. *Terry and the Pirates* opened with what sound?
a) a bell   b) a horn   c) a gong

5. Who starred in *A Man Called X?*
a) Herbert Marshall   b) Frank Lovejoy   c) Ned Sparks

6. What did Dunninger do for a living?
a) comedian   b) mentalist   c) singer

7. Who was not a character on *Life With Luigi?*
a) Pasquali   b) Goldberg   c) Horowitz

8. How did Wendy Warren begin her show?
a) doing news   b) singing   c) audience participation

9. Who hosted the Metropolitan Opera broadcasts?
a) Bill Cullen   b) Frank Knight   c) Milton Cross

10. Who was Mark Trail?
a) Conservationist   b) salesman   c) singer

ANSWERS

QUIZ #1   *(from page 1)*
1. Marjorie
2. Kate Smith
3. Bob Hope
4. Myrt
5. Black Swan Hall
6. Polly
7. George Jessel
8. Cheerios
9. Suspense
10. Parker Fennelly

QUIZ #2   *(from page 3)*
1. j
2. f
3. h
4. b
5. a
6. d
7. e
8. i
9. g
10. c

QUIZ #3   *(from page 6)*
1.   *Superman*
2.   *Suspense*
3.   *The Fat Man*
4.   *The Cisco Kid*
5.   *Mr. Keen, Tracer of Lost Persons*
6.   *Lights Out*
7.   *Captain Midnight*
8.   *The Romance of Helen Trent*
9.   *Inner Sanctum*
10.   *The Mysterious Traveler*

QUIZ #4   *(from page 10)*
1. b
2. e
3. g
4. h
5. a
6. i
7. f
8. c
9. j
10. d

QUIZ #5   *(from page 13)*
1. a
2. c
3. b
4. b
5. c
6. a
7. b
8. a & c
9. c
10. b

QUIZ #6   *(from page 15)*
1. True
2. False (They were brothers.)
3. True
4. False (She was a nurse.)
5. True
6. False (The longest-running sponsor was Blue Coal.)
7. False (His first name was Bill.)
8. True
9. True
10. True

QUIZ #7   *(from page 21)*
1. An adult western
2. He was a United States Marshall.
3. Chester Proudfoot
4. Parley Baer
5. Kitty Russell
6. She owned the Long Branch Saloon.
7. Doc Adams
8. Dodge City
9. Rex Koury
10. Norm MacDonnell

QUIZ #8   *(from page 24)*
1. e
2. i
3. b
4. j
5. a
6. g
7. h
8. d
9. f
10. c

QUIZ #9   *(from page 28)*

1. e
2. g
3. h
4. b
5. f
6. a
7. j
8. i
9. c
10. d

QUIZ #10   *(from page 33)*

1. Bob Elliott and Ray Goulding
2. WHDH
3. WOR
4. Piel's Beer
5. One Feller's Family
6. Wally Balou
7. The Two and Only
8. Mary McGoon
9. Mary Backstage, Noble Wife
10. "Write if you get work, and hang by your thumbs."

QUIZ #11   *(from page 36)*

1. Red-Blue
2. Silver
3. Orange
4. Lemon
5. Brown-Blue
6. Violets
7. Green
8. Pink
9. Yellow
10. Purple

QUIZ #12 *(from page 38)*

1. a
2. b
3. a
4. c
5. c
6. b
7. b
8. a
9. c
10. a

QUIZ #13 *(from page 43)*

1. e
2. g
3. h
4. a
5. d
6. j
7. i
8. b
9. c
10. f

QUIZ #14 *(from page 46)*

1. The drug store
2. The Ink Spots
3. *Lights Out*
4. Mrs. O'Reilly
5. Quaker Puffed Wheat and Quaker Puffed Rice
6. Jack Benny
7. Curley Bradley
8. George Fenneman
9. *The Sunshine Boys*
10. *The Jack Benny Show* and *The Phil Harris/Alice Faye Show*

QUIZ #15   *(from page 47)*

1. Ovaltine
2. He was an Aviator.
3. Monday – Friday, 5:30 (E.S.T.)
4. Decoders and Shake-Up Mugs
5. Albright
6. "The Secret Squadron"
7. Ivan Shark
8. Fury
9. Joyce and Chuck
10. Ichy

QUIZ #16   *(from page 48)*

RADIO:

1. *Mr. Keen*
2. *The Fat Man*
3. *Sam Spade*
4. *Nick Carter*
5. *Mr. Chamelion*

TELEVISION:

1. *Kojak*
2. *NYPD Blue*
3. *Law and Order*
4. *The Mentalist*
5. *Streets of San Francisco*

BOTH:

1. *Dragnet*
2. *Mr. District Attorney*
3. *Richard Diamond*
4. *Man Against Crime*
5. *Boston Blackie*

QUIZ #17 *(from page 51)*
1. d
2. f
3. a
4. i
5. c
6. g
7. j
8. h
9. e
10. b

QUIZ #18 *(from page 53)*
1. Dale Evans
2. Nellybelle
3. The Sons of the Pioneers
4. "Tumbling Tumbleweeds"
5. Riders of the Purple Sage
6. "Happy Trails to You"
7. Dale Evans
8. Dale's horse
9. Republic Pictures
10. "Goodbye, good luck, and may the good Lord take a likin' to you.

QUIZ #19 *(from page 57)*
1. Nick Carter
2. *Pat Novak, For Hire*
3. Erle Stanley Gardner
4. The Navy
5. *Terry and the Pirates*
6. Goodman Ace
7. *The Ed Sullivan Show*
8. Superman
9. Pepsi-Cola
10. Steve Dunne

QUIZ #20   *(from page 60)*

1. c
2. a
3. a
4. c
5. b
6. b
7. c
8. a
9. All three
10. a

QUIZ #21   *(from page 64)*

1. c
2. i
3. g
4. a
5. f
6. h
7. b
8. e
9. j
10. d

QUIZ #22   *(from page 72)*

1. d
2. i
3. g
4. j
5. c
6. f
7. e
8. h
9. b
10. a

QUIZ #23   *(from page 73)*

1. f
2. e
3. h
4. a
5. i
6. b
7. j
8. c
9. d
10. g

QUIZ #24   *(from page 74)*

1. j
2. d
3. a
4. g
5. h
6. c
7. b
8. f
9. e
10. i

QUIZ #25   *(from page 75)*

1. c
2. j
3. e
4. b
5. i
6. h
7. a
8. d
9. g
10. f

QUIZ #26   *(from page 79)*
1. True
2. True
3. False (He appeared on *Boston Blackie.*)
4. False (The star was Ann Sothern.)
5. False (He was the host of *Lights Out.*)
6. True
7. True
8. True
9. False (Suspense was on for twenty years.)
10. True

QUIZ #27   *(from page 82)*
1. c
2. b
3. f
4. g
5. i
6. j
7. a
8. e
9. h
10. d

QUIZ #28   *(from page 85)*
1. Winston
2. Camel
3. Philip Morris
4. Kent
5. Marlboro
6. Cool
7. Salem-Salem
8. Luckies
9. Raleigh
10. Chesterfield

QUIZ #29 *(from page 87)*

1. d
2. j
3. e
4. i
5. h
6. c
7. g
8. b
9. f
10. a

QUIZ #30 *(from page 92)*

1. *c*
2. *g*
3. *a*
4. *d*
5. *f*
6. *b*
7. *j*
8. *e*
9. *i*
10. *h*

QUIZ #31 *(from page 93)*

1. c
2. d
3. j
4. a
5. h
6. b
7. i
8. e
9. g
10. f

QUIZ #32   *(from page 96)*

1. William
2. Cristillo
3. Burlesque
4. Slapstick
5. *The Kate Smith Show*
6. Ted Collins
7. "Haeeey Abbott!"
8. "Who's On First?"
9. "I'm a Baaaad boy!"
10. *Buck Privates*

QUIZ #33   *(from page 98)*

1. True
2. True
3. False
4. True
5. False (It was Ken Carpenter.)
6. True
7. False (His dog was King.)
8. True
9. True
10. False (The station was in Detroit.)

QUIZ #34   *(from page 100)*

1. b
2. c
3. j
4. a
5. d
6. f
7. g
8. e
9. h
10. i

QUIZ #35 *(from page 104)*

1. a
2. b
3. c
4. b
5. a
6. c
7. c
8. b (all girls)
9. a
10. b

QUIZ #36 *(from page 106)*

1. Eddie Cantor
2. *Gangbusters*
3. Frank Sinatra
4. Andre Baruch
5. "Write if you get work, hang by your thumbs."
6. Kate Smith
7. Maxwell House Coffee
8. Cathy Lewis
9. Valentine
10. Jimmy Fidler

QUIZ #37 *(from page 108)*

1. Arthur Konan Doyle
2. The Fat Man
3. The Falcon
4. Pam and Jerry
5. Chick Carter
6. Mr. Chamelion
7. *Martin Kane, Private Eye*
8. Mr. Keen
9. Sgt. Joe Friday
10. Bulldog Drummond

QUIZ #38   *(from page 111)*

1. d
2. f
3. b
4. h
5. j
6. c
7. i
8. a
9. e
10. g

QUIZ #39   *(from page 113)*

1. True
2. False
3. True
4. False (The singer was Gordon MacRae.)
5. True
6. False (He starred in *Casey, Crime Photographer.*)
7. True
8. False (He was The Fat Man.)
9. False
10. True

QUIZ #40   *(from page 115)*

1. a & b
2. c
3. a
4. c
5. a
6. b
7. b
8. a
9. c
10. a

MEL SIMONS

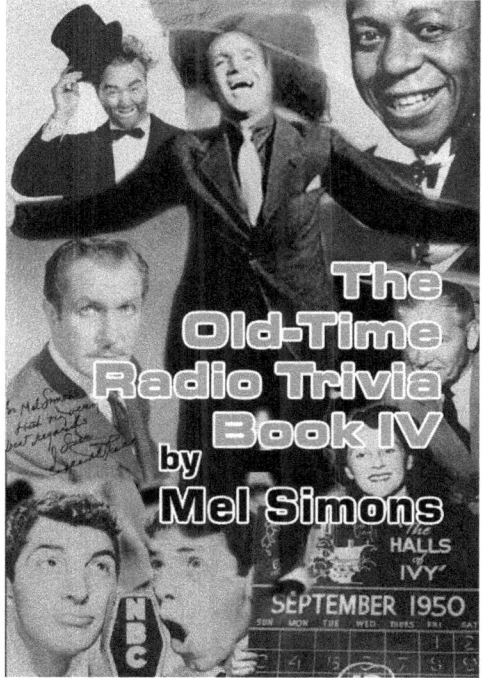

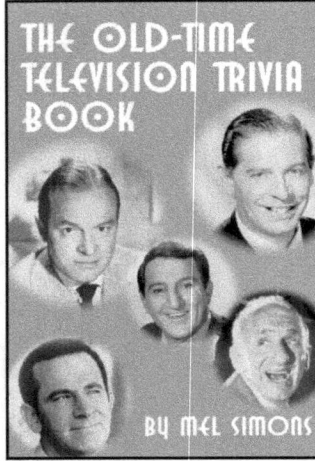

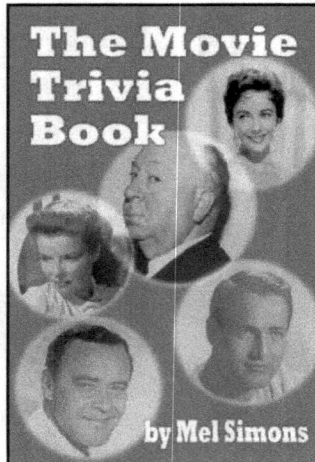

The Old-Time Radio Trivia Book
by Mel Simons

THE OLD-TIME TELEVISION TRIVIA BOOK
BY MEL SIMONS

OLD-TIME RADIO MEMORIES
by Mel Simons

The Show-Biz Trivia Book
by Mel Simons

OLD-TIME TELEVISION MEMORIES
by Mel Simons

The Movie Trivia Book
by Mel Simons

MEL

Available at bearmanormedia.com or at MelSimons.net

All just $14.95

E-books also
available!

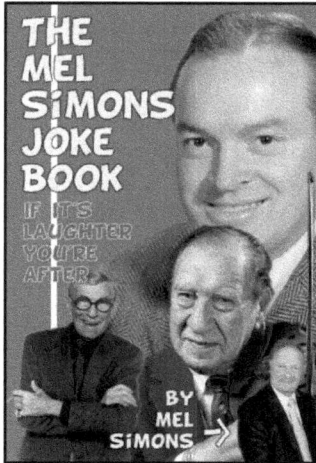

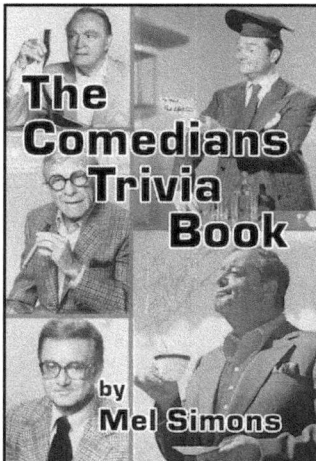

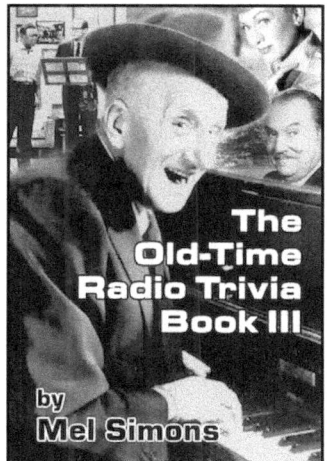

SIMONS

www.ingramcontent.com/pod-product-compliance
Lightning Source LLC
Chambersburg PA
CBHW071122090426
42736CB00012B/1979